TO REJUVENATE AND NOURISH

TO REJUVENATE AND NOURISH

NINE DAYS OF PRAYER TO ASKLEPIOS, GOD OF HEALING

GALINA KRASSKOVA

Copyright © 2016 by Galina Krasskova/Sanngetall Press

Sanngetall Press Valknot design by K.C. Hulsman

All rights reserved. No part of this book may be reproduced by any means or in any form whatsoever without written permission from the author, except for brief quotations embodied in literary articles or reviews.

CONTENTS

About Asklepios I
The Novena IV
   Day 1 V
   Reading for Day 1 VII
   Prayers X
   Offerings XIV
   Activity-Offering for Day 1 XV
   Closing Prayer XV
   Reading for Day 2 XVI
   Activity-Offering for Day 2 XVII
   Reading for Day 3 XVIII
   Activity-Offering for Day 3 XVIII
   Reading for Day 4 XIX
   Activity-Offering for Day 4 XX
   Reading for Day 5 XX
   Activity-Offering for Day 5 XX
   Reading for Day 6 XXI
   Activity-Offering for Day 6 XXI
   Reading for Day 7 XXII
   Activity-Offering for Day 7 XXIII
   Reading for Day 8 XXIII
   Activity-Offering for Day 8 XXV
   Reading for Day 9 XXV
   Activity-Offering for Day 9 XXVII
Bibliography XXIX
About the Author XXXI

This novena is offered in thanks to the God Asklepios, for His aid in helping my husband through surgery.

ABOUT ASKLEPIOS

Asklepios is the Greek (and Roman) God of medicine healing, and patron of the *Asklepiades*, or guild of physicians.[1] It is said that He invented several different types of healing and became so very skilled at His craft that He could raise the dead to life. He is the father of many skilled children, including Hygeia (health) and Panacea (cure-all). He shares the epithet of *Paian*, or 'Healer' with Apollo and several other Gods including Dionysos and Thanatos and His cultus was once spread throughout the ancient world.

Asklepios is the son of the God Apollo (Himself noted as a God of medicine) and the nymph Koronis.[2] In a tale that traveled from ancient Greece to the heights of Roman literature (Ovid's *Metamorphoses*), Koronis decided that she preferred a young human man over Apollo. When Apollo discovered this, thanks to the tattling of a raven, He asked His

---

[1] See the entry on Asklepios at www.theoi.com/Ouranios/Asklepios.html.
[2] Regional variants of His story give Him different mothers.

sister Artemis to kill her.[3] This Artemis did but Koronis went into labor as she died. Apollo saved the baby Asklepios at the very last minute by snatching him off the funeral pyre of his, the baby's, mother.[4] Perhaps regretting His hasty and angry actions in arranging for Koronis to be killed, his Father takes the child to the best of teachers, the wise centaur Chiron. There, Asklepios grows up learning divination, incantation, and all the different ways of healing. He becomes so skilled in the latter that He was reputed to be able to bring men back from the dead, an act against the natural order of the universe and one ultimately leading to His death: Hades, fearing that His hall would stagnate, never receiving new souls with Asklepios on the loose, asked Zeus to do something. Eventually, Zeus incinerated the Healer with a thunderbolt after which, He was raised up into the heavens,

---

[3] The story also provides an aitiology for why the raven is black. Apollo was so upset that He smote the raven, turning its feathers from their original pristine white to black.

[4] I have a tendency to use the Greek Apollon and the Roman Apollo interchangeably as they refer to the same God. The Romans acknowledged that they imported the cultus of Apollo during a time of sickness and plague.

taking His place both amongst the stars in the constellation Ὀφιουχος, the serpent holder, and also as a God on Olympus…with the caveat that He never again raise the dead save with permission from Zeus.

His healing temples dotted the Mediterranean landscape from Epidaurus to Kos (supposedly the birthplace of Hippocrates), eventually all the way to Pompeii and to Rome. Supplicants would undergo ritual purification and then offerings would be performed after which the patient entered the *adyton*, or sacred enclosure where they would spend the night. Any dreams or visions the patient might have would be interpreted by the temple healing-priests. The temples also housed healing serpents, which in some cases were allowed to range freely amongst the patients. In Rome, the Collegium of Asklepios and Hygeia was a burial society as well as a college of priests.[5] His particular symbol is the caduceus, or the staff twined with serpents and the snake is likewise sacred to Him. It is my hope to see His cultus spread once more in our modern world as we continue to restore our polytheistic traditions.

---

[5] See Carroll, p. 45-46.

THE NOVENA

A novena, from the Latin *novem* or 'nine,' is a traditional nine-day series of prayers. It was developed early on in Christianity as a devotional process whereby one might engage in an ongoing prayer cycle, either to petition for intercession or as an act of offering or thanks. The novena might be dedicated to the Virgin Mary, a particular saint, archangel, or other holy figure and there were rules established for the approval of specific prayers throughout the various Christian denominations that use them. We don't have that type of liturgical structure, but the structure of a novena is very useful and potentially a powerful way to immerse oneself in devotional prayer to a particular Holy Power, so I am repurposing it here.

The structure of this particular novena mimics the structure a patient might experience when visiting an ancient temple to Asklepios. Each night begins with ritual cleansing. Then there is meditation and prayer, finally the offering, and then one closes the cycle for the evening. Devotees should pay attention to their dreams during the novena cycle, and keep a record of any interesting dreams, visions, or omens received.

To begin, you will need an offering bowl or cup and nine tea lights. You may, of course, offer more, but this is the most basic requirement. Of course you will also need a place to make these offerings, either your own working shrine or a simple table or windowsill where they will remain undisturbed for the duration of your prayers.

DAY I

Begin this day and every day of the novena by cleansing yourself in some way. The easiest way to do this is by using a type of lustral water called *khernips*. This was, essentially, holy water and was used for cleansing prior to entering holy spaces in Greek polytheisms. The simplest version involves taking a bowl of good, clean water, lighting a couple of bay leaves, and dousing the burning sparking bay leaves in the water. Keep in mind as you do this that these things represent primal elemental forces, a union of opposites, balance, and purification and perform this action with ritual intent. You may even say something to the effect of, "May this water now cleanse and purify all it touches," or something similar. There are many ways to make lustral water, but this, I have found, is the simplest, and one of the most traditional.

Next, take a few moments—as many as you need—to get into the proper headspace. You are approaching one of the Holy Powers with your actions and with your prayers and it's important to be in the most receptive and focused headspace possible for that. This is a very special thing, a time set aside from the frenetic rush of your day. After you cleanse yourself, purifying away any miasma, sit for a few moments before approaching your shrine, altar, or wherever it is you have chosen as a focal point for your devotional work. Center yourself—the best way I have found to do this is by doing something called the 'four-fold breath.' It's very easy, since we all have to breathe and best of all you don't need any special tools. Begin by focusing on your breath and inhale four even counts, hold that breath for four even counts, exhale for four even counts, and hold for four even counts. Do this over and over for perhaps ten minutes.

Each day of the prayer cycle includes a suggested reading, upon which one might meditate. If you choose to include this in the nine day cycle, now is the appropriate time to do the reading and think about what it says about Asklepios, what you can learn from it, what hints it might hold as to His mysteries, how to approach Him, and the blessings He brings. Keep in mind that there are multiple regional variants of many of the readings and I have chosen the ones with which I am most familiar and which resonate most strongly with my own approach to Asklepios.[6] It is perfectly all right to substitute an alternate reading.

READING FOR DAY I

We begin our reading with a story drawn from Apollodorus (but also found in Ovid's *Metamorphoses*) describing the birth of Asklepios.

> "Likewise Leukippos was the father of Arsinoe. Apollon had sex with her, and she bore him Asklepios. Some say, however, that Asklepios was not born of Leukippos' daughter Arsinoe,

---

[6] I also tend to alternate indiscriminately between Latin and Greek spellings. Both Apollo and Asklepios received cultus in both Rome and in Greece. Apollo's (Apollon's) cultus came to Rome c. 431 B.C.E during a time of plague where He was reverenced as Apollo Medicus, or Apollo the Physician.

VII

but rather of Phlegyas' daughter Koronis in Thessaly. Apollon fell in love with her and immediately had intercourse with her, but she, despite her father's advice, preferred Kaineus' son Iskhys and lived with him. When a raven told Apollon this, he cursed it and turned it black in place of the white it had been before, and he killed Koronis. As she was being consumed on her funeral pyre, he snatched her baby fire and took him to the Centaur Chiron, who reared him and taught him medicine and hunting. As a surgeon Asklepios became so skilled in his profession that he not only saved but even revived the dead; for he had received from Athena the blood that had coursed though the Gorgon's veins, the left-side portion of which he used to destroy people, whereas that on the right he used for their preservation. This is how he could revive those who had died. Zeus was afraid that men might learn the art of medicine from Asklepios and thus help each other avoid death, so he hit him with a thunderbolt. This angered Apollon, who slew the Cyclopes, for they designed the thunderbolt for Zeus."[7]

---

[7] There is a lot wrapped up in this excerpt. Firstly, we see that even the ancient polytheists had difficulties accepting the attentions of their Gods—note how Koronis, like Cassandra before her, does not

(Pseudo-Apollodorus, Bibliotheca 3. 118–122, trans. my own after Aldrich.)

Once you have completed the reading and meditated for as long as you wish, offer one of the following prayers. These are the three prayers that you will choose from for the duration of the novena. You may switch them around, do each one for three days, or even write your own based on these. Use them as a guide and tool rather than an absolute. The important thing for this novena is that Asklepios receives nine nights (or days) of prayer.

---

necessarily reciprocate Apollon's affections. There is a Christian saying that ironically applies very well to devotional relationships: "it is a terrible thing to fall into the hands of the living God." Throughout the myths, our sacred stories, (especially in Ovid's retelling), Apollon is often thwarted in His love affairs and there is an element of both violence and tragedy in His affections. Likewise, we can see a strong parallel with the story of Zeus and Semele. As Koronis is burning to ash, Apollon saves Asklepios just as Zeus saved Dionysos from the burning body of Semele. There is an element of elevation here (more marked in Dionysos' double birth) that presages Their transformation into Gods.

PRAYERS

I. Prayer of Thanks

"I sing praises of You, Oh Mighty Healer, Glorious Son of Apollo and Your healing hands. I thank You for interceding in the fate and health of [insert name here[8]] and I pray for Your continued blessings and healing. Through You, Asklepios, I am [person x is] sustained. Through You, blessings are poured out upon the world. Yours is the power to restore. I pray fervently that You continue to extend Your mantle of health and healing over me [person x] and ever shall I continue to praise You. Hail to the God of healing. Hail to the wise counselor. Hail to the son of Apollon. Hail, Asklepios. Io."

II. General Prayer of Praise

"I praise the God Asklepios,
Wise and skillful Healer,
Son of Apollo,

---

[8] Adapt this and any of the proffered prayers to suit your own needs. If you prayed for your own healing, then say that; if you prayed for someone else's healing, simply insert their names in the relevant places. Change the prayer as you need.

and bright-hearted Koronis,
ever the friend of human kind,
ever compassionate.

Your caring touch relieves our pain,
Your skill restores our body,
and returns our minds to sense.
Oh God, best of healers, You sustain us.

With Your wise and caring daughters:
 Hygeia, the good goddess who inclines
our minds and hearts to self care,
gentle-handed Panacea, Who nourishes us
in our healing,
shining Aglaea, through Whose grace
we are uplifted,
firm and enduring Iaso, Who helps
us recover from wounds and illness,
cheerful Meditrina, Who helps us endure,
(and Who has the secret of salving balms)
fierce Aceso, Who stays the course,

and with Your sons,
skillful Makhaeon,
bane of poisons Poldalirius,
ever accomplished Telesphorus,
and those healing children
Whose names have been lost to time,

You teach us to life well,
You instill in us the principles of health,

self-care, and respect for the cycles of
life, healing, and death.

You ease our pain.
You guide our healing.
You strengthen our bones,
You salve our wounds –
be they of body, heart, mind
or spirit.

You are our spear and our shield
In our battles against maladies and afflictions.
You, most steadfast Healer, drive off the miasma
Of ill health and sickness, depression, fear,
and pain and Your skills are many;
beyond number are Your praises.

Aid us, I pray as we work toward health.
Encourage us in making healthy choices.
Encourage us in our stumbling path toward
Wholeness and healing.
Cleanse us of all pollution,
Oh Father of Physicians,
Ever willing to help humanity,
Ever willing to ease the damage we do,
The anguish we suffer.

I praise You, Asklepios,
Great God of Healing,
And I thank You,

For all Your gifts.

Hail."

III. Prayer for Healing

"Father of Healers,
most compassionate Asklepios,
Son of far shooting Apollo,
Best student of wise Chiron,
You Who are the swiftest of physicians,
Ever ready to restore the sick,
To mend our wounds,
To renew our health,
Please hear my prayer.

I know that through Your goodness,
Through Your merciful touch,
I might be healed of my pain and illness.
[Feel free to name the actual illness
from which you are suffering here.]
I know that through Your grace
and wise benevolence, I may be restored
to the fullness of vitality and vigor.
Favor my prayer, Oh kindest of Gods,
Look with mercy upon my affliction,
extend Your power over me,
and grant me healing, I pray.

Oh You Who have the power

to restore the dead to life,
to knit shattered bone together again,
to restore the breathe of being,
to drive back agony,
hear my prayer,
and grant me, I pray,
respite from this misfortune.

Hail to You, Asklepios,
Best and most skilled
Of healers."

OFFERINGS

Each day you will be asked to make a small offering: light a candle and pour out an offering. This offering may be clean fresh water, or it may be juice or wine. You may, of course, give other offerings (fruit, incense, flowers, etc.) too. At the very least however, water and fire should be given.[9] At this point in your nightly novena, light a candle and make that offering.

You will also be given a suggestion for something that you can do in the world as an

---

[9] Please do not think that there is anything wrong with offering water. It is the most basic offering and it is good. It is that which nourishes life and growth and it can and should be a staple in our offering repertoire.

active offering to Asklepios. You do not have to do this, but the suggestions are there in case you wish to or are able to (not everyone may be depending on health issues) make these offerings as well.[10]

ACTIVITY-OFFERING FOR DAY I

Go through your clothing and donate a couple of pieces to charity. (One of Asklepios' daughters is Aglaea, Who is numbered among the Graces, or the Kharites. It's from this that we get our English word 'charity.')[11]

CLOSING PRAYER

"May the good, gracious, and immortal Gods grant us the grace of love and trust in Their wisdom. May we ever praise and honor Them rightly and well and may we walk justly in Their favor. Hail to the Gods and Goddesses

---

[10] It may be that some of these active offerings are outside of your capability (either due to financial circumstances or health issues). In this case, should you wish to incorporate this into your novena, think about what you can do and feel free to adapt my suggestions or come up with something else all together.

[11] It comes to us through the Latin *caritas, -atis* which in turn draws from the same IE root as the Greek.

and tonight, hail especially to Asklepios."

Each night of the novena follows this structure:

1. Cleanse with khernips.
2. Do the reading given and meditate as directed above.
3. Say your selected prayer.
4. Make the offerings (every night offer a candle and at least water; the activity-offering is optional).
5. Read the closing prayer.

READING FOR DAY II

"I begin to sing of Asclepius, son of Apollo and healer of sicknesses. In the Dotian plain fair Coronis, daughter of King Phlegyas, bore him, a great joy to men, a soother of cruel pangs.

And so hail to you, lord: in my song I make my prayer to thee!"[12]

---

[12] Asklepios comes by His skill for healing naturally. Apollo Himself is praised as 'medicus,' or healer, and in

(The Homeric Hymns, translation by Hugh G. Evelyn-White.)

ACTIVITY-OFFERING FOR DAY II

Donate time or money to a healing charity of your choice.[13]

---

the *Iliad*, we see Him taking an active role in the Trojan War, first and foremost by avenging his priest (who was mocked and shown disrespect by Agamemnon and whose daughter was held captive by the warlord) via a terrible plague, which He set upon the Greeks. He is here called Apollon Smyntheus, or Apollo of the Mouse…the mouse being a creature that, like rats, may carry fleas that can cause sickness and plague. So Apollon too is a healer and like any healer may bring blessing or bane. Even today, physicians having completed their training take the Hippocratic oath, where they swear by "Apollo the Physician and by Asklepios and Hygeia…."

[13] My favorite is Paralyzed Veterans of America, but there are numerous charities and non-profits that raise money and awareness and help fund the search for cures. There is a good list here: www.thelifeyoucansave.org/Where-to-Donate, that covers not only health, but also clean water, nutrition, and sustainable agriculture.

READING FOR DAY III

"Of the various Aesculapii the first is the son of Apollo, and is worshipped by the Arcadians ... The second is the brother of the second Mercurius [Hermes]; he is said to have been struck by lightning and buried at Cynosura. The third is the son of Arsippus and Arsinoe, and is said to have invented the use of purgatives and dentistry. His tomb and grove are shown in Arcadia, not far from the river Lusius." [14]

(*Cicero, De Natura Deorum 3. 22, my translation after Rackham.*)

ACTIVITY-OFFERING FOR DAY III

Commit to working out, be it on your own or by joining a gym, at least twice a week. (Asklepios has a daughter named Hygeia, Whose area of expertise is all about preventive care. Getting regular exercise helps keep the

---

[14] This shows how widespread and varied the cultus of Asklepios was in the ancient world. Cicero is wrestling here with regional variants, sometimes huge variants, of Asklepios' divine origins. It really highlights how popular His cultus was across the ancient Mediterranean.

heart and joints healthy, which contributes to our overall good health. This seems something right up Her alley.)

READING FOR DAY IV

"Apollo took the child Asklepios to the Magnetian Centaur Chiron, that Chiron might teach him to be a healer for all mankind of all their maladies and ills.

All then who came to Him, some ill with plague, some with sores and festering growths, some wounded by the strokes of bright-bronze weapons, or by the stone shot of slings, others with limbs ravaged by summer's fiery heat or by the winter's cold, to each for every ill he made the appropriate remedy, and gave deliverance from pain, some he cured gently with songs of incantation, others by means of soothing draughts of medicines, or by wrapping their limbs around with doctored salves, and some he made whole by means of the surgeon's knife."

(Pindar, *Pythian Ode 3. 45, my translation.*)

ACTIVITY-OFFERING FOR DAY IV

Donate non-perishable food items to a local foodbank, or donate two hours of your time to a local soup kitchen.

READING FOR DAY V

"The god [Apollon] can not only save life but is also the begetter of Asklepios (Asclepius), man's saviour and champion against diseases."

(Aelian, On Animals 10. 49, trans. Scholfield.)

ACTIVITY-OFFERING FOR DAY V

Put together five care packages (in a large, gallon sealable plastic bag, put tissues, aspirin, nutrition bars, feminine hygiene products, toothbrush, toothpaste, soap, deodorant, warm socks, etc.) and give them out to local homeless. This takes a bit of guts and boldness, but it's a project that we've been running in my town for a year now and it seems to be well received. Obviously, if you include feminine hygiene products (and they're expensive, so frankly, I would) be sure to give those bags only to women! Do this with compassion – it is just a turn of luck that has put that person on the street and not you and not me.

READING FOR DAY VI

"To Apollon and Koronis (Coronis) was born Asklepios (Asclepius), who learned from his father many matters which pertain to the healing art, and then went on to discover the art of surgery and the preparations of drugs and the strength to be found in roots, and, speaking generally, he introduced such advances into the healing art that he is honoured as if he were its source and founder."

(*Diodorus Siculus, Library of History 5. 74. 6, trans. Oldfather.*)

ACTIVITY-OFFERING FOR DAY VI

Plant a medicinal garden and learn the medicinal uses of at least five herbs. Make offerings of these to Asklepios and His children.

Or go and clean up a local park. Pick up trash for a couple of hours.

READING FOR DAY VII

"Iarkhos led back the argument to the subject of divination and among the many blessings which that art had conferred upon mankind, he declared the gift of healing to be the most important. 'For,' said he, 'the wise Asklepiades [i.e. the ancient guild of doctors reputedly descended from Asklepios] would have never attained to this branch of science, if Asklepios had not been the son of Apollon; and as such had not in accordance with the latter's responses and oracles concocted and adapted different drugs to different diseases; these he not only handed on to his own sons, but he taught his companions what herbs must be applied to running wounds, and what to inflamed and dry wounds, and in what doses to administer liquid drugs for drinking by means of which dropsical patients are drained and bleeding is checked, and diseases of decay and the cavities due to their ravages are put an end to. And who,' he said, 'can deprive the art of divination of the credit of discovering simples

> which heal the bites of venomous creatures, and in particular of using the virus itself as a cure for many diseases? For I do not think that men without the forecasts of a prophetic wisdom would ever have ventured to mingle with medicines that save life these most deadly of poisons.'"
>
> (*Philostratus, Life of Apollonius of Tyana 3. 44, trans. Conybeare.*)

ACTIVITY-OFFERING FOR DAY VII

Adopt a nursing home patient who has no family. Volunteer your time at a nursing home to read to the elderly.

READING FOR DAY VIII

> "Sing, oh young people, of Paean[15], Leto's son,

---

[15] One of the praise names of Asklepios, it has also been applied in Homeric texts to Apollo and several other Gods. It may have originally referred to a Minoan healing God Whose cultus was absorbed by the enormously popular Apollon and likewise transferred to His son.

renowned for His skill, of the Far-shooter—*ie Paian!*—who fathered a great joy for mortals when he mingled in love with Koronis in the land of the Phlegyai—*ie Paian!*—

Asklepios, the most famous god—*ie Paian!*

By him were fathered Makhaon and Podalirus and Iaso the healer, —*ie Paian!*—and fair-eyed, radiant Aglaea, and Panakea, Whose healing hands cure all, children of Epione, along with Hygeia, the all-glorious goddess of health, vibrant and undefiled;

ie Paian! Asklepios, the most famous god—*ie Paian!*

Greetings I give to You: graciously visit our broad and spacious city—*ie Paian!*—and grant that we look on the sun's light in joy, with the approval and help of Hygeia, the all-glorious, undefiled.

— *ie Paian!*—Asklepios, the most famous god—*ie Paian!*" [16]

---

[16] This is a fascinating praise poem. Typically in ancient Greek epic poetry, and in fact, in ancient Greek writing in general, a son is known by his father. Hence one will often see, for instance, a hero named followed immediately either by 'son of X' or by the

(*Inscription from Erythrai, Fragments 939, Greek Lyric V, my own translation.*)

ACTIVITY-OFFERING FOR DAY VIII

Write your own prayer to Asklepios. If you have a blog, consider publishing it there.

READING FOR DAY IX

"Healer of All, Asklepios, Lord Paian,
You enchant away the misery of suffering men.

---

father's name in the genitive case, which shows that the son belongs to the lineage of the father. In *Bacchae* for instance, this is so marked that Pentheus is often referred to by an adjectival variant of his father's name (Echion), as the 'Echious one,' whenever he is most strongly demonstrating his father's less than laudable personality traits Here, however, it is Apollo, in the by-name "Paian" who is being praised for having fathered a son so wonderous as Asklepios. It is a juxtaposition of the normal way of things, one that points to the power and benevolence of Asklepios and His cultic popularity. I will admit, that I'm not exactly certain whether "Paian" here refers to Apollo, Asklepios, or first One and then the Other. Even in the original, it's rather uncertain (both are masculine vocatives).

Come, Mighty and Soothing One, lead us back to health,
and stop our sickness and the harsh fate of death.
You, Blessed Helper, bringer of growth,
Who restores all to blossoming wholeness,
You ward off evil,
Mighty and honored Child of Phoebus Apollon.
Enemy of disease, Whose partner is blameless Hygeia,[17]
Come, Oh Blessed One, Savior, granting a good end to life.

(Orphic Hymn to Asklepios, my translation.)

---

[17] Every Orphic group had its own independent mythology which they adapted from the better known Homeric and Hesiodic versions. Here, for instance, Hygeia is the partner (literally consort or bed partner) of Asklepios and not His daughter. This reflects not only regional differences, but what we might term denominational differences in the sacred mythos of this God. One can see the same thing with the mythic cycle of Dionysos. In the better known stories, His Mother is Semele, but there are likewise stories, where it's Persephone and other Goddesses, depending on the region have been named as well. This may be confusing but I think it is best accepted as a mystery and that the important thing is honoring Them.

Charming, Lovely, Blossoming, Queen of All,
Hear me, Blessed Hygeia, Bringer of prosperity,
Mother of All, for through You the illnesses tormenting mankind
Vanish, and through you, every house blossoms into the fullness of joy,
And the arts prevail and flourish. The cosmos yearns for You, Lady,
And only lethal Hades always loathes You;
Ever youthful, ever desired, Repose of mortals.
For apart from You, all is pointless for humanity;
Apart from You, the giver of abundance, and wealth, sweet to those who feast, fails, for man never comes into long-suffering old age,
For of all things, You alone are sovereign and Queen.
But, Goddess, come ever a Defender to initiates,
And draw away the ill-fated distress of harsh disease.

(Orphic Hymn to Hygeia, my translation)

ACTIVITY-OFFERING FOR DAY IX

Donate blood if you are able.

Conclude the final day of the novena with the following prayer:

> "All praise to Asklepios and to His illustrious family. May my prayers be pleasing to You now and always. Hail, Asklepios and all Your children. This novena is formally ended, and I thank You."

BIBLIOGRAPHY

Aelian. *On the Characteristics of Animals.* (3 volumes.) Translation by Schofield, A F. Loeb Classical Library. Cambridge, MA: Harvard University Press.

Apollodorus. *The Library of Greek Mythology.* Translation by Aldrich, Keith. Lawrence, Kansas: Coronado Press, 1975.

Carroll, Maureen. *Spirits of the dead: Roman funerary commemoration in Western Europe* Oxford: Oxford University Press, 2006.

Cicero. *Nature of the Gods, Academics.* Translation by Rackham, M A. Loeb Classical Library. Cambridge, MA: Harvard University Press.

Diodorus Siculus. *Library of History.* Translation by Oldfather, C H. Loeb Classical Library, Volumes 303, 377. Cambridge, MA: Harvard University Press.

Greek Lyric V, New School of Poetry and Anonymous Songs. Translation by Campbell, D A. Loeb Classical Library Vol 144. Cambridge, MA: Harvard University Press.

Hesiod, the Homeric Hymns, Epic Cycle, the Homerica, Translation by Evelyn-White, H G. Loeb Classical Library Vol 57. Cambridge, MA: Harvard University Press.

Ovid. *Metamorphoses*. Translation by Melville, A D. Oxford: Oxford University Press.
Pindar. *Odes*. Translation by Conway, G S. Everyman's Library.

Unless otherwise noted, original Greek taken from Perseus Digital Library available here: http://www.perseus.tufts.edu/hopper.

Sources accessed in translation at theoi.com; see entry for Asclepius.

ABOUT THE AUTHOR

Galina Krasskova is a polytheist, Heathen, and priest of Odin. She practices both Heathenry and cultus deorum and blogs regularly at http://krasskova.wordpress.com. She is the author of numerous books on the Northern Tradition, holds a Masters degree in Religious Studies, and has done extensive graduate work in Classics. She is currently pursuing a graduate degree in medieval studies.

XXXII